MX 8733300 7

CW01614740

H[illegible]art-Davi[illegible]

WITHDRAWN

MX 8733300 7

[illegible]chnic Library

Joni Farthing

OUT OF THE IN-TRAY

Acknowledgments

The idea for this book came from a management training exercise in A A Zoll's *Dynamic Management Education* published by Addison-Wesley Publishing Co 1966. Thanks are due to James Dixey for bringing this book to my notice and to students of the English Language Teaching Unit at Christ Church College, Canterbury for their helpful suggestions during testing.

First published in Great Britain 1982 by
Hart-Davis Educational Ltd., Frogmore,
St Albans, Hertfordshire.

Copyright © 1982 Joni Farthing

All rights reserved. No part of this publication may be reproduced, stored in a retrieval system or transmitted in any form or by any means, electronic, mechanical, photocopying, recording or otherwise without prior permission of the publishers.

ISBN 0 247 13149 0

Printed by Martins Press Limited, London EC1R 0EN

Names of organisations and persons central to each chapter of this book are fictitious in every case. Resemblance to existing persons or organisations is purely coincidental.

Granada ®
Granada Publishing ®

SITE HE	MIDDLESEX POLYTECHNIC LIBRARY
ACCESSION No.	8733300
CLASS No.	651.75 FAR
SPECIAL COLLECTION ✓	

By the same author

BUSINESS MAZES

Contents

Introduction

What is an in-tray?

On your office desk you probably have two trays or baskets. One holds correspondence that has just arrived, and the other holds correspondence that is ready to leave you. The first is an in-tray or in-basket, the second an out-tray or out-basket.

How to do an in-tray exercise

There are five 'in-trays' in this book, designed to introduce and practise language common in business situations. They comprise either individual items from an in-tray, or a complete file on a specific problem. In each exercise you must read the correspondence and decide how to deal with it. This may involve writing letters, memos or a report, talking to colleagues or making phone calls. Sometimes there will be items that you cannot deal with immediately. In these cases, decide what information you need and where to get it. Some items you may simply pass to someone else in the office.

If you are working through an in-tray in a group, it is important that you discuss each item fully before deciding how to deal with it. Practise your English by putting forward ideas and listening to those of your group.

There will be a time-limit for you to complete the exercise. If time is short, run quickly through all the items marking those that need special attention. Underline phrases that sum up the item or will need discussion in the group. If you have enough time, make quick notes on the items to remind you what you think about them before the group starts its discussion. Remember to leave time for any writing that needs to be done.

If you complete the in-tray exercise before the rest of the class, go back over the items and note the new words and phrases you met. Notice how letters begin and end and why some sound more formal than others. All this will help you when you write your own letters in English.

Notes to the teacher

These 'in-tray' exercises are designed for good intermediate and more advanced students. The exact level depends on how much vocabulary is pre-taught, how much individual help you can give while the students read and discuss, and how much time is available. The in-tray exercises are suitable for students learning English for business purposes, but they can also be used with other adult learners.

Aims

The students will become familiar with the style of English letters and other written communications, and will learn to read and use vocabulary and structures relevant to business correspondence. They will improve their ability to think and discuss in English and develop letter-writing skills. If a short time-limit is set for the exercises, the students will develop the skill of skim-reading, that is, very fast reading for essential information only. This is a much-needed skill that is often lacking because students may look upon every piece of written English as an exam paper!

For additional oral practice, a short role-playing exercise is suggested after each in-tray. A written assignment is also included to practise letter-writing.

Teaching plan

1 Explain the aim of the lesson, eg fast-reading, vocabulary building, discussion practice, or a lead-in to letter-writing work.
2 Ask the class to read the Introduction on page 4.
3 If necessary divide the class into pairs or groups of up to four.
4 Select one of the in-tray exercises and set a time-limit.
5 Move between the students ready to help with language difficulties immediately.
6 When the time is up, ask each group to select a speaker to explain how his group dealt with the correspondence and why they made their decisions.
7 Encourage some generalisation towards the end of the discussion by asking what they felt were the underlying problems in the situation, and what improvements could be suggested. Encourage the students to support their views by using phrases from the in-tray exercise.
8 (optional) After a break, ask the students to prepare the role-playing exercise. Again, move around the classroom and help with language problems. Role-plays can be acted out just for the group itself or to the class as a whole. They can be video-recorded or audio-recorded, corrected and improved and re-recorded.
9 (optional) Set the written assignment for homework.

1

DR BARKER'S IN-TRAY

The situation

You are secretary to Dr Caroline Barker, head of the herbicide research unit at Ostwith Centre for Agricultural Studies. Dr Barker is giving an important lecture at the moment and afterwards she will only have ten minutes to see you before she leaves for a conference in Bonn, Germany, where she will be until April 3rd.

It is your job to go through Dr Barker's in-tray. Deal with as many items as you can and then decide what to do with the rest. Write out the memos you will send, make rough drafts of letters and make notes on any phone calls to be made. List the items you will hand to Dr Barker before she leaves and note any decisions you will ask her to make before she leaves for Germany – but be sure that anything you ask her to do immediately will not take longer than ten minutes.

18th March 198-

To all academic staff

Please note the new regulations governing claims for travel and accommodation expenses.

1. Form TR 31 (blue) will be replaced by forms TR 32 (yellow) and PTR 33 (green) as from 1st April.

2. Copies of forms TR 32 and PTR 33 should be obtained from the Bursar's office <u>before</u> staff incur expenses.

3. Staff should obtain full receipts for all expenses incurred as detailed on form TR 32. Receipts should be attached to a completed TR 32.

4. TR 32's should reach the Bursar no later than 3 pm on the 22nd of the month in which the claim is to be paid. Late claims cannot be paid until the end of the following month.

5. Staff obliged to live away from their normal place of residence for more than three consecutive nights, not including Sunday nights, may claim a provisional interim payment of not more than £50, or two thirds of the estimated expenses whichever is the less, by submitting a completed form PTR 33 to the Bursar before leaving. In exceptional circumstances emergency provisional interim payments may be made by post at the discretion of the Bursar.

6. All claims up to and including those expenses incurred on March 31st should be made on form TR31. All expenses incurred after that date should be claimed on the new forms TR 32 and/or PTR 33.

T. J. Yates
Bursar

Senior School
0297-435987

Mayland,
Crossfield Park,
Little Broughton,
West Sussex HO8 6TR

17th March, 198-

Dear Dr Barker,

I was so sorry you could not be present at the Old Maylanders reunion last term but I was fascinated to hear that you were pursuing research in South America. I am sure everyone at Mayland would love to hear more about your work and it is with this in mind that I am writing to you now.

As you probably remember from your own schooldays, it is the tradition at Mayland to invite an Old Girl to speak at Prize-giving each year. It would be a great honour to the school and give our girls a true sense of pride if you would accept our invitation to speak this year.

The girls profit so much from hearing of the achievements of their predecessors. We still have an excellent reputation for producing science scholars and among fifteen girls who gained University places in a science subject we had two accepted at Girton and even sent an engineer to Imperial College last year. However, science is still so often thought of as a man's domain. I know your career would serve as a fine example of the fact that women can get to the top too, and it is on this theme that I would particularly like you to speak.

Prize-giving this year will be held on July 7th. I am sure you will appreciate that I have to make final plans immediately after the Easter holidays and that therefore a reply to our invitation by the beginning of April would be very helpful.

I do hope you will be able to accept,

With very best regards,
Yours sincerely,

C. Coalthorpe-Morton

Cynthia Coalthorpe-Morton
Headmistress

TELEPHONE MESSAGE

Date: Mar. 18 Time: 9.20

Call for: Dr. B Call from: Alan

Message:

Weather conditions affecting herbicide 95/L/4 tests. Halt application?

Please call X

Please call urgently

Information only

Caller will try later

TELEPHONE MESSAGE

Date: Mar. 18 Time: 9.50

Call for: Dr. B Call from: Husband

Message:

Please call

Please call Home urgently X

Information only

Caller will try later

Mowbray Finch International
New York London Sydney
186 Park View, Walthamstow, London E17 2LT
Telephone: 01-599 0101 Telex: 898989 Mow Int.

Our ref: GLB/DJ

Date: March 198-

THE GREAT LAND SCANDAL by MARIA BROOKES

Dear Sir/Madam

It is not my policy to recommend books personally to readers, but in the case of THE GREAT LAND SCANDAL by MARIA BROOKES I felt I had to make an exception.

Here at last is a book that opens the cupboard door on the skeleton of international land prices. Acclaimed by academics and critics alike as a breath-taking exposé of the secret wealth of Europe's land-owners, THE GREAT LAND SCANDAL will demand a place on every informed reader's bookshelf.

Open your eyes to what is arguably the most shocking disclosure the world of agriculture has ever known, by ordering your copy of THE GREAT LAND SCANDAL by MARIA BROOKES immediately. 294 pages packed with all the up-to-date facts and figures on international land ownership and prices. After this truly exceptional volume you will survey the softly rolling Downs and the towering snow-capped Dolomites with different eyes.

THE GREAT LAND SCANDAL by MARIA BROOKES is the one publishing event of the year that you just cannot afford to miss. And ordering could not be easier. If you have any difficulties obtaining THE GREAT LAND SCANDAL by MARIA BROOKES from your local bookseller simply fill in the form below, tear off, and post direct to me.

Greg Bannerman
Editor

- -

Please rush me my copy of THE GREAT LAND SCANDAL by MARIA BROOKES. I understand that if I am not shocked by the contents I can return it within seven days and obtain a full refund.

Name ....

Department ....

College/University ....

I enclose cheque/postal order for £7.95 plus £1.65 postage and packing.

CHAPEL AND BRIGHTON EDUCATIONAL PUBLISHERS LIMITED

P.O. Box 6, Python House, Broad Street, London W1A 2NH
Telephone: 01-443 4444 Telex: 494345 Cable: Python

Dr Caroline Barker
Herbicide Research Unit
Ostwith Centre for Agricultural Studies
Greenham
Ostwith Cheshire

17th March 198-

Dear Dr Barker

Many thanks for your comments on Chapters 5-10 of An Introduction to the Control of Grassy Weeds in Corn and Soybean Crops. These have all been transferred to the original typescript.

Our designer has produced a rough layout of the text, and I'll send you samples when it is in a more complete form. He has made a line drawing of a clump of weeds with a fist held tight around them. It looks very effective and the idea of the control of weeds is thus reflected on the cover. We will get a copy of this design made and I will send it to you for your approval.

We are now considering the back cover of the book. On publications of this type we like to put a photograph of the author together with a very short, informal biography. Would you send a photograph which you feel would be suitable, and write an outline of your career, perhaps including educational details and a word or two about your family? Don't worry too much about length at this stage. We can make any alterations and, of course, send them to you for your comments.

Yours sincerely

James Gore-Millard

James Gore-Millard
Editor, Science and Technology

University of Vindeln,
Department of Agriculture,
Sveavägen 197,
Vindeln,
Sweden,
March 15th.

Dear Dr. Barker,

Thankyou for the up-dated bibliography you sent me last month. There are a few things on it I'd like to get hold of. The library here is very efficient so there shouldn't be any problem.

Meanwhile, however, I wonder if I could come and see you some time soon. I'm afraid the results I'm getting here have suddenly changed quite dramatically. I've checked everything but still don't have much idea of what the cause is. The only thing I can think of is the effect of winds we've been getting here over the last week or two. I don't really see why strong winds should make much difference but there doesn't seem to be anything else to account for the recent results.

I'd like you to go through my figures with me on the K2L tests and see if you can shed any light on the problem. As you know I've accepted a research post with Massandra starting in September and I don't want to find myself with an unfinished doctorate on my hands at that stage.

I'll be in England between the 24th and 31st March. Could you give me a tutorial appointment sometime then?

Apart from the K2L results (!) everything is going fine. My skiing has improved enormously and I'm actually beginning to look forward to fish for lunch every day here in college!

Yours,

Brian L.

84b Gladstone Mansions,
London N6.

Dear Caroline,

March 17th.

Hope this reaches you before you leave for Bonn. Just wanted Brian Lawler's address in Sweden. He's still attached to you at OCAS isn't he? With Harry getting posted to the Middle East in September I thought I'd just take the kids and find somewhere peaceful in the country to live for a year. That leaves 84b empty. Brian mentioned last summer he was going to need a place to live when he got back and I thought I'd do us both a favour and give him first refusal on it. (Hope he can afford it, they pay pretty generously these multinational companies don't they?) Anyway I'll have to get him to look over it and fix a rent with him soon or someone else is bound to ask me. So if you've got a moment do let me have his address.

Have a good time in Bonn and give me a ring when you get back,

Yours, Joanne

P.S. Did you hear Jeremy got married again! You'd have thought he'd have learnt his lesson by now wouldn't you!

OCAS and SOLAS

The Library

Dear Colleague,

17. 3.

As term draws to a close I should like to remind you that you have on loan 12 books.

I should be grateful if you would return those books you have finished with as soon as possible, and check with a member of the library staff the titles you wish to renew.

Yours sincerely

L.H. Forbes

L.H. Forbes
Tutor/Librarian

27, Frogmore Way,
Hampstead,
London NW3

17th March

Dear Dr Barker,

I am applying for a post with the Potato Marketing Board. May I use your name as a reference? I'm sure they will send you details of the job but, briefly, it involves research into the French maincrop potato marketing system. If I got the job I'd be able to use some of my Coronphema experience.

To bring you up to date since I left OCAS, I've married (I don't know if you remember Bill, I brought him along to a couple of dos at the Unit) and now have a lovely son, Gareth, which is why I've been keeping so quiet for the last two years.

By the way, I saw your article on PR94 in JAAS the other day. It sounds like you've make quite a breakthrough.

Yours, with best regards,

Eileen Phillips
(née Henderson)

MASSANDRA AGRICULTURAL PRODUCTS

are pleased to announce

LARGO

---

the new post-emergent, nonselective herbicide that controls the broadest spectrum of problem weeds. (EPA approved)

As a leading authority in the field of agriculture MASSANDRA AGRICULTURAL PRODUCTS invite you to hear more about *LARGO*'s outstanding performance over lunch at the Crown Prince Hotel, Grosvenor Square, London W1 on May 2nd at 12.30.

R.S.V.P. by April 17th to Ms A. Long, Room AP414, Massandra House, Knightsbridge, London SW3 1WK.

Dear Member

As you probably know Miss Eleanor Grigson is getting married over Easter. She has now worked at OCAS for over four years as Dr Barker's secretary and I am sure you would like to show your appreciation for her friendliness and help over that time, and to send her your best wishes for her future happiness, by donating something towards a wedding present. If we collect enough we would like to buy her a dinner service as the Christmas dinner last year showed she was quite a cook!
Please let Celia Farnham have your donation by Friday March 21st.

Pauline Cooke,
Secretary S.C.R.

The Dr Barker role-play

Aim: To practise apologising and expressing interest
Roles: Dr Barker and Miss Cynthia Coalthorpe-Morton
Scene: A telephone conversation between Dr Barker and Miss Coalthorpe-Morton about the invitation to speak on Prize-giving Day. (See page 9.)

Act out the telephone conversation:

Dr Barker explains why she will not be able to speak at the Prize-giving but asks a number of questions to show that she is still interested in her old school.

Miss Coalthorpe-Morton has already been rejected by other speakers and is desperate to persuade Dr Barker to attend. She may offer a good lunch and overnight accommodation, remind Dr Barker of her obligations to her old school or promise to buy all her books for the school library. Or she may ask her to find another Old Maylander to step in and do the job instead.

Decide on Dr Barker's age and school achievements and add any interesting details you think are appropriate. Ask a lot of questions and be as polite as possible.

The Dr Barker written assignment

Imagine you are Dr Barker and your secretary is leaving today to get married and move to Canada with her new husband. Write a brief letter on behalf of the staff to accompany the gift that will be presented to her later today.

Here are some phrases you may find useful:

This small gift comes with our very best wishes for ...
We all wish you and your future husband ...
We hope you will accept ... in appreciation of ...
You will be missed by ...

2

THE ARTS SPONSORSHIP FILE

The situation

You are Sandra Austin. You have recently started work as public relations officer with Fairbrother Ltd. Fairbrother is a company which owns and runs a small chain of supermarkets in the south of England.

Your first job is to decide how to use the £5,000 available for arts sponsorship. This is the first time Fairbrother has set aside money for such sponsorship. Your predecessor, Max Redmond, has left you the file he built up on the problem and you are expected to make a quick decision based on the contents of this file. It is now 9am. You should look through the file on the following pages, make your decision and write a brief report giving your reasons. Your report is to be presented to the directors of the company at 11am. (If the suggested two-hour limit is allowed, take a short break before beginning to write your report.)

CONFIDENTIAL

NOT TO BE REMOVED FROM THIS OFFICE

Sandra,

Here are a few remarks that may help you make up your mind on the sponsorship question. I trust you will treat them as confidential.

1. Charles Fairbrother, the MD, has just heard that his eldest son has been accepted at the Slade School in London to do a further two years study as a painter. Alex has already been studying art at Maidstone College for the past three years. C.F. is very pleased, which could account for the decision to put £5,000 into the arts.

2. Brian Stonehouse, Marketing Manager, who has been responsible for 'upping' the Fairbrother image over the last five years, has told me he feels we should support local opera to stress the fact that we are a company with class!

3. There's a packer in the warehouse at Dover, Jack Saunders, who has been with the company for years. I'm told he has a daughter in a local dance company. * See letter from her

4. When Gary Harry, the buyer for greengroceries, heard about the sponsorship idea he phoned me to say he hoped we were not going to give 'punks' money. By punks I think he implied those artists who did not drive a car or have a house mortgage!

5. The Ashford branch cashiers called a special meeting about the idea. They were very enthusiastic about it and said they thought the money should be spent on educational projects, as in this way some of their children might be helped.

6. Apart from Charles I don't have any information on the interests of the other board members. Presumably none of them are particularly interested in painting or sculpture as nobody has ever bothered about buying anything to decorate the boardroom or the directors' offices. Charles, of course, has hung a couple of his son's things in his room.

Max R.

THE TEMPORARY DANCE COMPANY

58A Rothermere Studios, Rothermere St.,
London SE13. Tel: 01-586 4389

Mr Max Redmond
Public Relations Officer
Fairbrother Ltd
72-74 Francis House Lane
Canterbury

February 15th

Dear Mr Redmond

The Temporary Dance Company was founded in 1976 to bridge the gap between the small 'workshop' companies and the large national companies. We have established a first-class reputation both in Britain and abroad and continue to dance to packed houses throughout the year.

We are anxious to establish Residencies in various areas including the South East. A Residency involves the company giving a number of stage performances backed up by numerous workshops and visits to schools, colleges and arts centres in the area.

One week's Residency, in Canterbury for example, would cost £2,500. If you would like to offer sponsorship for such a Residency we will be happy to discuss details of advertising your sponsorship. In addition, your staff would get concessions on seats at all our performances during the year.

Yours sincerely

Rodney Cockburn

Rodney Cockburn
Finance and Public Relations Officer

The One-Eye Mime Group
c/o The Shakespeare Theatre
High St
Dover

January 20th

Mr Max Redmond
Public Relations Officer
Fairbrother Ltd
72-74 Francis House Lane
Canterbury Kent

Dear Mr Redmond

My father is a packer in the Dover warehouses of Fairbrother's and has told me that you are thinking of donating some money to an arts project in this area.

The One-Eye Mime Group, of which I am a member, is totally unsupported by any public or private body. We are very popular in the South East especially with students and young people, but in spite of good attendances we are getting into debt and have not paid full salaries for the last three months.

I do hope you will help us as without a local sponsor we will probably have to disband. Any amount would be acceptable and, of course, we would make sure you got Fairbrother's name in all the local papers and on the local radio as the media love to report our activities.

Best wishes

Mimi S.

Mimi Saunders

N.B. They do get a lot of press coverage — but mainly because their shows are so outrageous !

M.R.

Notes on other companies' experiences of arts sponsorship

January 198-

Albion Bank Ltd

Give annual national literary prizes for published novels and short stories. Support national opera. No immediate rewards expected or received but they feel arts sponsorship is a 'trust-builder' and will continue but not expand. Would not disclose annual sponsorship budget, but literary prizes amount to about £3,000 and possibly the opera costs them £15,000-£20,000.

British Wholefoods

Similar chain to Fairbrother but more specialised in natural health foods market. They said they sponsored anything for the under 30's e.g. opera, youth orchestras, drama festivals etc. They believe they reach the right public but think sponsorship takes years to act as a successful image-builder and expect no immediate pay-off. They will continue and possibly expand. Said budget varied according to profits but refused to give figures.

Mainline Superstores Ltd

Big, national chain of department stores. Used to sponsor art exhibitions and bought a great deal of painting, prints and sculpture. Have stopped in the last year. "You can't make anything on it. People just expect you to give more and more. Our customers don't know a Hockney from a Holbein but they do know the difference between iron and non-iron shirts and that's what matters in the end", commented their PR man when I phoned him. They will lend their art collection to galleries but have otherwise dropped out of the arts.

Karina Dancewear

Medium-sized company manufacturing and retailing dance and gymnastics clothing. Sponsored national and local ballet and modern dance festivals last year and are very pleased with the results. Said they managed to make some mutually profitable deals with dance companies as a result, and felt they had got their name across very successfully to thousands of amateur dancers and their mothers. Expect a sizeable increase in trade next year as a result. Budget around £6,000 last year and will increase it this year and next.

Kingsgate Motors

The only local firm who seemed to spend more than £1,000 annually on arts sponsorship. This car-hire and car-sales company spent just over that figure on underwriting the Christmas pantomime at the local Canterbury theatre. Said they would probably continue out of kind-heartedness but that it brought no rewards.

from the annual report given on March 14th last year

The past year has shown a marked change in profits. After making the difficult decision to close three of our outlets in industrial areas of falling employment for which we saw inadequate longer-term profit potential, we saw a rise in overall profitability of the Company. This reflected the steep rise in the volume of sales of imported food and wines.

This has proved to be an important year in the Company's history as it has shown the very real change in customer from the wife of the unskilled industrial worker, who accounted for 80% of our trade in our first year of operation, to the young middle-class career couple, who accounted for approximately 60% of our custom last year. It is now the goal of management to reach a higher level of profitability by supplying our public with an even wider selection of quality food products. We will also upgrade the shopping environment for our customers by extending two of our stores, installing improved lighting in some others and changing all in-store music transmission to soft popular classics.

It is our intention to pass on the benefits of higher profits by improving staff conditions. This will include the adoption of new uniforms and the provision of creche facilities in at least three of our branches. We are happy to announce an increased bonus to all staff, and hope to continue this rise in the coming year.

...n he finishing ...ud sigh of dis- ...om the crowd, ...through to set and the fourth ...the world this

...lit new fires of escape from the ...resence of Coe ...im") and Ovett ...ble") at 1,500 ...new distance, ...adjustment of ...tics will bring ...y in the Com- ...es 5,000.

...contest there ...ama to embar- ...selectors. Geoff in the 10,000 ...ay night in 28 ...eason's fastest narrowly mis- ..., while three Julian Goater

...n Smith—and ...l is the wrong ...ing the 10,000 ...ater made no ...sh a fast last ...'s race, which ...he Cup, but if ...he form he ...s an offi...

... himself past Willi... Gault and Rod Milburn into third position in 13.75, his best of the season.

Stop Handouts to Arts

Speaking at the opening of the Royal Academy Summer Exhibition yesterday, Mrs Frieda Friedman-Lewis, Minister for the Arts, urged business to take more financial responsibility for the arts in Britain. She criticised companies for not making more use of the advertising potential offered by arts sponsorship whilst making clear she felt it was not the job of central government to give 'handouts' to artists.

It is extremely difficult to claw back from such a bad start without making a mistake and while it needs a touch of luck, Holtom's talent and strong, ... approach ... him

...broken and ... straight, to a ... appointment fr... Coghlan went ... an Irish record ... fastest time in ... year.

Walker has ... hope. He can ... dominating p... ("I can't beat ... ("He's vulnera... metres, into a ... knowing that ar... training and ta... reward, probab... monwealth Gan...

Behind this was another d... rass Britain's Smith, second ... metres on Frid... 8.7, ran his ... 5,000 in 13 26.33, ... sing third place ... places back was in 13 29.07.

He is the ma... many others—fe... one to be runn... in Zagreb. Go... attempt to spla... lap into Saturday ... he will need in ... he is not in ... should be, then (in Her Majesty's and a gentlema...

Sandra,

In case you don't have time to go through all the figures on customer profile, I've jotted down a few of the more relevant statistics so that you've an idea of what kind of people shop at Fairbrother.

<u>Age</u>	58% of customers are aged between 18 and 30 30% of customers are aged between 31 and 50
<u>Sex</u>	37% of customers are male
<u>Occupation</u>	75% of customers aged under 21 are full-time students 72% of all other customers are in 'middle-class' (ABC) jobs.

5 Gladbrooke Studios,
Callforth Gate,
London E17.

February 20

Public Relations Manager,
Fairbrother Supermarkets,
72-74 Francis House Lane,
Canterbury,
Kent.

Dear Sir,

I am exhibiting some recent paintings at Canterbury Community Centre in August. These paintings will be of special interest to you and your company as their theme is mass-produced food. I am therefore writing to you to ask for some help towards the cost of a catalogue and posters for the show. I think £2,500 would cover it.

As you know, local arts associations and community centres have very little money to pay for such things these days since the Conservatives took over and cut their budgets. I interviewed Alex Fairbrother, whom I believe is your M.D's son, for a course at the Slade and he ~~has~~ mentioned his father was keen to spend money on the arts. I was very pleased to hear that, at last, private business is going to do something for the arts.

Yours, Jack Mack

SOUTHERN ARTS GROUP
The Regional Arts Association
for Kent and East Sussex

80 Crescendo Road Maidstone Kent MD1 2SA Telephone: (0622) 91875

President: Lord Gravesend
Chairman: Lord Peter Rook
Director: Helen Palmer

Mr Max Redmond
Public Relations Officer
Fairbrother Ltd
72-4 Francis House Lane
Canterbury
Kent CA9 4LS

February 8th

Dear Mr Redmond

In reply to your request for information on arts sponsorship in the South East, I am pleased to draw your attention to the enclosed list of schemes administered by SAG. I hope you will wish to invest in one of them.

Among the benefits you can expect from your investment are free advertising space in programmes, special booking terms for your staff and mention of your sponsorship in all publicity. Should you wish for more details about any of these schemes and how they can benefit your company I will be pleased to discuss them with you.

Yours sincerely

Kevin Prebble

Kevin Prebble
Deputy Director

SOUTHERN ARTS GROUP BUSINESS SPONSORSHIP OPPORTUNITIES

LITERATURE PRIZES

SAG offers a prize of £1,000 for the best work of fiction of the year by a writer living in South East England. Sponsorship is sought for a similar annual prize for the best work of non-fiction.

ART PURCHASE SCHEME

SAG can offer up to 50% subsidy on works purchased for public display. Free professional advice is available so that a sound investment may be made. £1,000 will purchase a painting or sculpture by a young artist who shows the potential of making an international name in the art world. £5,000 will purchase a major painting or sculpture by a nationally known and respected artist.

YOUNG MUSICIANS CONCERTS

A competition is held each year to find the best young musicians in the country. The winners are offered a regional tour starting in London. £75 will sponsor a recital outside London by one musician. £200 will sponsor the London debut of one musician. £1,000 will sponsor a regional tour of one winning musician.

MEMO

To Max Redmond, PR **Date** January 8th

From C.F.

It is my feeling, and also that of the other directors, that the company should be doing something to bring our name more into the public eye by sponsoring 'worthy causes'.

My preference is definitely for the arts, which do not seem to get much of a deal these days from public funds.

Can you look into this and present a short report of your findings and a recommendation we can discuss at the directors' meeting on March XX, 11a.m.

See if you can come up with something that will promote our up-market image with people in the area and help some artist or group that really needs help. You could ask around the company too, and get a few opinions on the subject.

Budget for around £5,000 for next year. We do not want to commit ourselves to anything long-term until we see how the first year turns out.

1 Ramsden Cottages
Eastry
Nr Dover
Kent

March 18

Public Relations Dept
Fairbrother Ltd
72-74 Francis House Lane
Canterbury
Kent

Dear Mr Redmond

A group of artists living and working in Kent is organising a show of its recent work. The exhibition will be held at the Ramsgate Gallery and will run from June 6 to July 7.

The organisation of the exhibition has unfortunately coincided with a decision by the local Education Authority to withdraw their financial support for all art in the county except for the two art schools.

In view of this decision, which will mean many fewer people in Kent will be able to see art in the future, we wish to make the exhibition reach as large an audience as possible. To do this we would be grateful for any financial assistance you can offer us. The SAG is able to offer £300 towards hire of the gallery and security staff. We would like to ask you for £150 towards the cost of printing a small catalogue, and £100 towards the cost of insuring and transporting the work.

I hope you can help us in this.

Yours sincerely

M. Poland

Michael Poland

SOUTH EAST OPERA

Canterbury School of Music,
Townfield Place, Canterbury,
Kent CA4 7AA Tel: 0227-7575

20 January

The Public Relations Officer
Fairbrother Ltd
72-4 Francis House Lane
Canterbury

Dear Sir

After last year's highly successful season, performing everywhere from church halls to major concert halls, South East Opera is now rehearsing its new repertoire for the coming year.

As always at this time we write to local and national firms to ask for sponsorship towards the costs of the company. Sponsorship last season allowed us to bring opera to some 30,000 people in the South of England. And even more than this number saw the sponsor's name on the thousands of posters advertising our performances. In all the programmes sponsors were allowed liberal advertising space, bringing their name to the notice of our audiences.

To enlarge our touring plans this year and allow us to reach at least 50,000 people we desperately need more financial assistance. A total of £10,000 is needed, although, of course, any help will be greatly appreciated.

If you would like to hear more details of SEO please contact me immediately.

Yours faithfully

Candy McClaggan

Candy McClaggan
Finance Officer

The arts sponsorship role-play

Aim: To practise the language of formal, ordered discussion
Roles: The Chairman of the board and any number of directors of Fairbrothers, Sandra Austin, a secretary (optional)
Scene: A meeting in the boardroom to discuss Sandra Austin's report on arts sponsorship

Choose one report to be Sandra Austin's. Everyone in the group reads it and decides whether they agree with it. Now act out the meeting:

The first item on the agenda is the report on arts sponsorship. The Chairman opens the meeting and introduces Sandra Austin. She reads her report to the board and discusses it with them. The Chairman should control the discussion, put forward his own ideas and sum up at the end. He should decide whether to impose a time limit on the discussion and whether or not there will be a vote. If a secretary is present he should take notes of the discussion and ask for points to be repeated if this becomes difficult. The directors may make suggestions but these should be convincing. Discussion can be 'through the Chair' if the Chairman wishes.

Remember that only Sandra Austin has the complete file on the subject.

The arts sponsorship written assignment

Write a letter to the artist or group who will receive sponsorship from your company. State how much money you are offering and any terms or conditions affecting its use. Finally invite the artist or representative to lunch to discuss the matter further.

Here are some phrases you may find useful:

I am pleased to inform you that ...
On behalf of ... I would like to offer you ...
We are particularly concerned that ...
... and in return we expect ...
We hope you will agree to ...
I would like to discuss ...
I would like to meet ... over lunch on ...

3

THE PAYNE PAPER BAG AND PRINTING COMPANY

The situation

You are Michael Payne, owner-manager of M Payne Ltd, manufacturers of paper bags, and printers of paper bags and stationery. Your staff includes:

Kenneth Pitts (aged 55)	Production supervisor for 15 years and your deputy when you are out of the office.
Catherine Miller (aged 30)	Your secretary for two years.
Colin Mason (aged 23)	Bookkeeper and general office assistant for eighteen months.
Fred Parry (aged 64)	Storeman for sixteen years. He retires in a couple of months.

The company employs a total of forty-two staff, most of whom work in the factory. The others work in the office, or as outside sales staff.

You have been on holiday in Kenya for the past fortnight and have promised to look into the office quickly today, Sunday June 25th, before you leave for the next two weeks of your holiday visiting relatives in Australia. Look through the contents of your in-tray and decide what, if any, action to take on each item. Remember to leave clear notes for your staff if you want them to do anything. You should not try to phone staff at home unless it is the only way of dealing with a problem. Prepare details of exactly what you will do with any matters that can wait until you get back from Australia.

To Mr Payne **Date** 19th June
From Colin

MEMO

The Fairfax order is one week behind schedule. They are threatening to cancel. There was an initial hold-up because we were waiting for that special ink they wanted. But the ink was delivered four days ago and the order still hasn't been run off yet. I've mentioned the Fairfax complaints to Ken, but ....

Mike,

Have a look at this note I found pushed through the letter box on Thursday morning. Fortunately I found it before anyone else came in. I haven't said anything to poor Mrs. Worth, but should I contact the police?

Ken

I've seen you in church Mr. Payne and I know you are a good Christian. Well you want to watch that 'Mrs' Sylvia Worth. She steals things. Believe me, I know. Did you know she'd left her husband and baby and lives with another man, for instance?

BLONDELL AND SONS LTD.
32 High Street, Cheadle, Cheshire   Tel: 477 5959

SUPPLIERS OF FRUIT AND VEGETABLES TO THE DISCERNING

The Manager
M. Payne Ltd
Dray Road
Manchester 16

19th June, 198-

Dear Sir

You supplied us with 10,000 white sulphite paper bags on June 12th. My staff have had to put up with complaints from customers who say the bags are falling apart. This is true, I tested a few myself and almost all of them were badly glued along the sides.

I phoned you this morning and your secretary told me you were away. I also talked to Mr Pitts but he seemed determined to do nothing. I can assure you I will never do business with your company again, and will make sure nobody else along the High Street does either, if I don't receive an apology and refund within 24 hours.

Yours faithfully

F.G.H. Blondell

F.G.H. Blondell
Manager

To Mike **Date** 15th June

From Ken

MEMO

Molly Turner is on one of the 529 folding machines. She refuses to pin her hair back. I think it's a real safety risk as it is. Any ideas? I wouldn't like to get rid of her as she's a nice girl.

To Mike **Date** 14th June

From Ken

MEMO

That special order for Macdonald Chocolates for 4×2 greaseproof paper bags isn't working out. We've done about 100 and I've noticed the glue isn't sticking on the new plastic coated paper. The order's due on July 3rd. Shall I tell them we can't fulfil it?

To Mr. Payne **Date** 14th June

From Colin

MEMO

A couple of people have phoned about personal stationery. I thought we didn't do short runs and said no. But Ken says we should never turn away custom and wants me to get back to them. Quite honestly I'd rather have your agreement first.

WILLIAM SHAKESPEARE COMPREHENSIVE SCHOOL
Abbeyfield Street, Manchester 9.   Tel: 448 9077/8/9

The Manager
M. Payne Ltd
Dray Rd
Manchester 16

14th June 198-

Dear Mr Payne

The group of boys and girls who visited your factory on June 12th have all said how interesting and enjoyable their visit was. One boy, in particular, was so interested in what he saw that he is going to write his careers project on the paper-making and printing industry. Such visits to local companies help our young people to make informed decisions about their careers after school, which is so important in these days of employment difficulties.

It was very good of you to allow us to look around your factory, and of your staff to show us how everything worked. In particular I would like to express my thanks, and those of Class 5C, to Mr Kenneth Pitts, who gave up so much of his valuable time that afternoon. He even stopped one or two of the machines to let the children have a go at working them. I am aware that such things cost a company time and money and wish to say, therefore, how very much we appreciated his efforts to interest the children.

Yours sincerely

John Mortimer

John Mortimer
Careers Adviser

Have a look at this order. Can't trace
Tidmes at all in the books. No address,
nothing. Do you know who took
this order?

Ken

/

NAME Tidmes

ORDER No. 8342 MACHINE 8

SIZE 7×7 ~~PLAIN~~/PRINTED

PAPER No. 1 Sulphite

QUANTITY 100,000 ~~NOT~~ STRUNG

COMPLETED .... SIGNED ....

6 SAMPLES REQUIRED

PROMISED
Date for June 30th

To Mr Payne **Date** 18th June

From Colin

MEMO

I can't get a straight answer out of Ken. Are we giving the kids their outing to the seaside again this summer? If so, are we going to use our own cars again, or are we going to hire a coach as we discussed last year? I know you'll be in a rush this weekend when you come in, but could you just say yes or no on both things. I must book the coach next week or we'll miss out.

To Mike **Date** 18 June

From Ken

MEMO

Remember that unwanted order of white sulphite bags from the Spence St. Bakers that we advertised last month? A chap called Blondell bought the whole batch of 10,000. He rang up this morning. Very rude to Cath and to me. He's complaining they're badly glued but he's a greengrocer. He must have been putting potatoes in them – no wonder they came apart!

I don't reckon we owe him a thing. He saw the bags before he bought them. I told him this but he wouldn't accept it. Do you want to do anything?

23 Parswood Close,
Sale,
Cheshire,
17th June

M. Payne Ltd.,
Dray Rd.,
Manchester 16.

Dear Mr. Payne,

I am a student at Higham College of Art, studying graphic design. I wonder whether you have any vacancies over the summer? I am looking for a job over the vacation, any time between July 1st and September 20th. I'm willing to do anything, especially if it is connected with printing. I am keen to learn about industrial printing.

My father, Stephen Turner, suggested I get in touch with you as he knows you from St. Thomas' choir.

Yours sincerely,
Jonathan Turner

Friday

Mr Payne,

I thought I'd better let you know Mrs Worth in the canteen was late again today. That makes 3 out of the past 5 days everyone has had to wait till almost 12 for their tea. Everyone seems to blame <u>me</u>, but <u>I</u> can't tell her to get in earlier.

Cath

Friday

Mr Payne,

Could you leave your O.K. on these holiday dates.

Frank Patterson		June 19-July 2
Myra Moynihan		August 21-Sept 3
Hilary Wooley	)	
Mandy Fry	)	
Pauline Jones	)	August 7-20
Joan Finch	)	

I've checked these against the other dates you've already said yes to. No problems except that the packing section is going to be understaffed in August because Hilary, Mandy, Pauline and Joan want to go on holiday together. That just leaves Carol. Could we move Molly Turner for those two weeks? She's on folding but says she's sick of it.

Cath

To Mike **Date** 17 June

From Ken

MEMO

Bit of a crisis. Jack mis-read an order of 3,000 as 30,000. Should have checked of course but too busy with you away. Anyway, we've printed up 27,000 too many letterheads for Continental Meat Carriers. Haven't said anything to them yet as I thought I'd wait for your decision.

Mike

Can you tell Ken Pitts to hurry up about despatching the Continental Meat Carriers order. I haven't got room for it in the stores, as he well knows.

Fred

To Mr. Payne

From Colin

Date 17th June

MEMO

An order for headed writing paper has been over-run. It'll mean quite a loss if we just get rid of the extra. Here's what we could do:

A) Offer the extra (27,000) to the customer at a large discount.

B) Guillotine the heading and advertise the smaller sheets at a discount.

C) Store the extra and hope the customer re-orders.

D) Guillotine the heading and cut into four, to sell as scrap pads.

Would you O.K. one of these or add your own thoughts so that I can get moving on this. It seems to be upsetting Fred Cosgrave in the stores!

The Payne role-play

Aim: To practise speaking firmly but tactfully
Roles: Michael Payne and Mrs Sylvia Worth
Scene: A discussion about Mrs Worth's personal problems in relation to her work

Look at the two items involving Mrs Worth, from Ken and from Cath (pages 34 and 40). Michael Payne has decided to speak to Mrs Worth so that the morning tea will not be late in future.

Imagine that Michael Payne is not leaving immediately for Australia. He calls Mrs Worth into his office on Monday morning to talk to her about her poor time-keeping. Decide whether he will warn Mrs Worth, threaten her with dismissal, talk over her home situation etc. Mrs Worth is expecting the talk to be about her being late over the last few days. Decide what excuse she will give, whether she will tell the truth, whether she will get upset easily or give the impression that she is not interested in her job at Payne's. Decide on the details of Mrs Worth's employment, how long she has worked for the firm etc. Add any small details that make the talk interesting.

The Payne written assignment

Write a letter in reply to Mr Blondell's complaint about the paper bags. Be polite but do not offer him a refund.

Here are some phrases you may find useful:

In answer to your letter of . . .
I was very sorry to hear from your letter of . . .
Please accept my apologies . . .
I regret the inconvenience caused but . . .
I am sure you appreciate that . . .
In the circumstances I'm afraid . . .
I must remind you that . . .

4

THE FINDORP IN-TRAY

The situation

You are a sales engineer in the industrial pump division of Findorp Ltd. A colleague has been rushed to hospital and your sales manager has asked you to go through his in-tray and deal with any urgent matters you find.

The sick colleague, John Morrison, is Findorp's northern representative for industrial pumps. He usually works from an office in his home, which is where you are now, looking through his correspondence. His job is to sell pumps to industries in the north of England. He makes regular visits to old and potential customers, advises them on pumps suitable for their needs, and sends details of their requirements to Findorp's tendering department so that accurate quotations can be given. He sends firm orders to the works manager so that manufacture can begin, and keeps his customers informed of progress. He also informs his sales manager of matters which might affect the formulation of Findorp's sales policy.

The items in John Morrison's in-tray are reproduced on the following pages. Decide how you will deal with each item and write notes on your decisions. If possible draft replies to letters and pass information on to colleagues. If there is any material you cannot handle yourself, note down what you will do with it.

Directors:
H. D. Blunt (Chairman)
K. Wit (Managing)
R. R. Line (Dep.)
F. Bithel
G. White
G. T. Dillons

ENDPOINT ENGINEERING LIMITED

A member of the Cressholt Group of Companies
Registered in England No. 659993
Endpoint House, Widnes WD4 7GH

Telephone: Widnes 47634
Telegrams: Endpointwid
Telex: 665079

Order No. C453/46
In all communications refer to the above no.

To: Findorp Ltd Bowtree House Piccadilly London W1A 6AK	Date: 4th October 198- Job: C 747
Delivery address: Endpoint Engineering Ltd. c/o Standstead Paint Co. Ltd., Stoneygate Lane, Wrigham, Blackpool, Lancs	Advice notes: To Head Office: 2 With Goods: 2 No. of invoices required: 1
No. of copies of certified drawing required: 2 (URGENT)	Delivery dates: Goods: End November Drawings: End October
No. of instruction manuals required: 2	Your contact in connection with this order is: G. Faber

Conditions of Contract:

The contract is to be carried out in accordance with G.T.E.'s "General Conditions of Order" Form 100B. No waiver or variation of these conditions or any conditions included in your acceptance shall be binding unless the same has been specifically agreed in writing by us.

Please supply and deliver, carriage paid, to the above address:

18 - Centrifugal Pumps in accordance with your telex quotation reference 1986 dated 8 July.

Total fixed price: £9,780.00

This price is fixed for the duration of the contract and includes delivery to the site.

Terms of payment: Net cash monthly account

Please acknowledge this order immediately

For Endpoint Engineering Ltd.

K. M. Mason

Manager Contracts Division

Gruber Industrial Pumps

Gruber Dean House, Hill Road, Basildon, Essex BS1 1AC
Telephone: 0268-452 4545   Telex: 605549

7th October 198-

Mr J.W.Morrison
54 The Heights
Village Green Place
Wilmslow
Cheshire

Dear John

I managed to squeeze a bit extra out of Ronald Mitchell as he understands why I'm so keen to get you to come over to Gruber. This means that our final offer stands at £18,000 basic plus commission terms identical to your present payments from Findorp. In addition I've been authorised to offer you 50% extra commission on all orders you can divert from Findorp. Of course we'll see your car is one grade up from your present one, and we'd like to give you the option of living rent-free in one of our 6-bedroom, executive houses in Colchester. I think your wife might like that. That all adds up to a lot more than you are getting at the moment as far as I've heard. Think about it over the weekend. Talk to your wife. Tell her about the house. She can come down and look it over if she likes. I don't think you'll say no again John.

Let me have your answer next week.

I look forward to welcoming you to Gruber.

Regards

Laurie

Laurence Kale
Sales Manager Europe

Salesman's Report

Company Visited A. A. Pumps (Distributors) Location Manchester

Names and Titles of People Interviewed Fred Crane — Director

Date of Visit 28th Sept.

Subject of Report Possible order for 2 off M40-150-150T

Report Written by John Morrison

Jack

As usual, Fred needed a pricing concession urgently and in your absence I OK'd him to offer his customer 2 off M40-150-150T at the old price — Fred still had to give the customer 15% discount owing to competition from Anstley-White. If I had insisted on the extra 5% I think AA Pumps would have lost the job. Anyway those 2 off M40's have been on the stock list long enough — it must be worth 5% to us to say goodbye to them!

Now all I have to do is make sure Fred gets his order — and places it with Findorp.

Regards,

J. M.

John M. — O.K. provided AA's customer places the order in October. Let me know as soon as he does so that I can alert the Contracts Department.

Jack Stone 7/10

5/10 10.05 HRS S.C.

SENT 11.00 HRS

691348 FDLDN G

484399 CRILPL G

3756 FINDORP TX 691348

SALES DEPT

PLEASE ADVISE IF YOU CAN SUPPLY WATER DRIVEN PUMPS. IF YES
PLEASE SEND LITERATURE ETC TO UNDERSIGNED AT -

C.R. INDUSTRIES LTD, GREYHOPE INDUSTRIAL ESTATE, LIVERPOOL 9.

REGARDS, K.S. THOMPSON C.R. INDUSTRIES, LIVERPOOL

484399 CRILPL G
691348 FDLDN G

Salesman's Report

Company Visited SLANT ENGINEERING Location PORTSMOUTH

Names and Titles of People Interviewed L. COOPER – PROJECT ENGINEER

Date of Visit 4 OCT.

Subject of Report GRUBER PUMPS

Report Written by STEVE DREISER

I understand from the above that Gruber have recently launched a new pump size (equivalent to our KL55) within one of their present ranges.

The selling price of this unit is 30% (on average) below our list price.

Gruber did a major promotion of their new product at Slant Eng. (part of Cable World Ind.).

I could not pick up any of Gruber's official literature or more details but suggest the department could ask distributors for more information.

Note this – KJ/HS/HW/GC/JM and let me have reports as soon as possible.

J. E. Stone

4th October, 198-

MEMORANDUM

To: K.L. Jeffreys, London H Stanton, Home H. Wrigley, Home
G.L. Collier, Home J.W. Morrison, Home S. Dreiser, Home

From: J.E. Stone, London

- -

Gentlemen,

<u>Bookings</u>

Are you checking your monthly computer bookings reports? Please confirm.

J. E. Stone

J.E. Stone
Sales Manager, Industrial Pump Division

YOUR CUSTOMER TELEPHONED TODAY

Mail to: JOHN MORRISON Date: 6/10

Name of Caller: DOUG HYMES Position Held:

Company: PALIN CORP Nature of Business:

Address: FARLEIGH GREEN IND. ESTATE, PRESTON, LANCASHIRE.

Telephone No.: (0772) 500712

Details of Call: LABOUR DISPUTE ON SITE.

POSSIBILITY OF VANDALISM. CAN PALINCORP

DELAY DELIVERY OF PUMP (DUE 2ND. DEC.)

FOR COUPLE OF MONTHS?

✓ Please call back as soon as possible/~~before~~

Appointment needed

Verbal/Written quotation

Technical information given

Sales Literature sent on

Parts List sent on

YOUR CUSTOMER TELEPHONED TODAY

Mail to: JOHN MORRISON Date: 7/10

Name of Caller: MR. ARNOLD Position Held:

Company: CAIRNS ENG. Nature of Business:

Address: FALLOWFIELD RD., DARNLEY, NR. BOLTON

Telephone No.: (0204) 586349 X7

Details of Call:

URGENT

WANT TO ALTER ORDER

DUE 29TH NOVEMBER.

✓ Please call back as soon as possible/~~before~~

Appointment needed

Verbal/Written quotation

Technical information given

Sales Literature sent on

Parts List sent on

Period Sept / Oct
Representative J. Morrison

Orders Booked In

Order No.	Customer	Due on Site	Commission
2052097	Gainmore	18/10	✓ normal
2052156-8	L. Brand	15/11	✓ normal
2052169-75	"	23/11	✓ special
2053020 - 30	Cairns Engineering	18/10	✓ special
2053031	"	1/11	✓ special
2053032 - 34	"	29/11	✓ normal
2054137 - 38	Palincorp	25/10	✓ special
2054139 - 45	"	28/10	✓ special
2054146 - 47	"	2/12	✓ special
2054148	"	5/2	✓ normal
2054149	"	22/6	✓ normal
2057633	Plantnorm	28/11	✓ normal
2057800	R.S. Grant	3/5	✓ } special
2059116 - 19	"	21/7	✓ } special

These commissions OK'd for payment
Oct. 25th
J. E. Stone

CAVANDISH
PUMP
DISTRIBUTORS
LIMITED

Firth Street, Oldham OL3 2ER
Telephone: 061-610 4994 (6 lines). Telex: 523169

Our ref PLC/SF
Your ref
Date 6.10.8-

Findorp Ltd.
Industrial Pump Division
Cleethorpes
Lancashire

<u>For the attention of Mr. J. Morrison</u>

Dear John

Accept my apologies for the delay in replying to your letter of 8th September but as you will appreciate the decision to accept the Findorp pump distributorship for this area is not a simple one for either of our companies. However most problems have now been resolved and the only outstanding worry on our side is the limited range of stainless steel pumps Findorp would permit us to stock.

No doubt you will have heard of the interest shown in this area by K.R.S. of Salford and we are now awaiting the revised terms they can offer us. As soon as we have their firm proposals we will be in a better position to make a decision on whether to accept a full or part distributorship from you. Should you reconsider your terms for supplying stainless steel pumps in the meantime, please let me know.

Yours sincerely

Peter C.

P.L. Cavandish Managing Director

Directors P. L. Cavandish, J. S. Cavandish, M. Leyton
Registered Office as above Registered in England No. 304962

7/10 11.58 HRS L.H.
SENT 2.15 HRS

691348 FDLDN G

57233 BIBMCT G

4113 FINDORP TX 691348

ATTN. J W MORRISON

PLEASE SUBMIT QUOTATION FOR FOLLOWING

PUMP

LIQUID	BUTANE
TEMP (MAX/MIN)	20 DEG C/0 DEG C
SPECIFIC GRAVITY	0.50
VISCOSITY	0.17 CP @ 0 DEG C
CAPACITY	65 TE/HR
HEAD	90FT
ELECTRICAL SUPPLY	4 15 CV/3PH/50HZ
NO OFF	2

IN ORDER THAT A TRUE ASSESSMENT OF YOUR QUOTATION CAN BE MADE
PLEASE SUBMIT ALL RELEVANT DESIGN DATA AND MATERIALS OF CONSTRUCTION

REGARDS
J O HOLLINGSWORTH

PROJECT ENGINEER

57233 BIBMCT G

691348/FDLDN G

FOR THE ATTENTION OF J.E. STONE

Listed below (A) are orders where production control have advised they are unable to meet the requested despatch date. This is either due to the non-availability of pump parts or it is due to the late delivery of B.O. equipment.

List (B) = no change to requested despatch date.

LIST A

Order No.	Delivery Request	Del. Delay
2053023	for 18.10	3 weeks
2053024	for 18.10	3 weeks
2053025	for 20.10	3 weeks
2079421	for 18.10	1 week
2079422	for 22.10	2 weeks
2084393	for 25.10	(Minimum 12 weeks)
2054146/7	for 2.12	(Minimum 12 weeks)

LIST B

Order No.
2053020/1/2
2053026
2053027
2053028
2053029
2053030
2065976
2065977
2079427
2079428
2079429
2085976
2086831

For information to —
201 K. Jeffreys
202 H. Stanton
205 J.W. Morrison
206 S. Dreiser
207 H. Wrigley
208 G. L. Collier

Date Completed: 7/10

Signed F. L. Widney
Contracts Department

11 Monday	9.30. Jerry Brown, K.S. Industries. Discuss quote. 12.00. Alan Klein, Palincorp. Get information on new project. Lunch? PM Ring Jack Calder, Baramco Tubes. Get appointment with him and M.D. for next week.
12 Tuesday M's birthday tomorrow. Earrings? Watch?	9.00 ↓ H.Q. Product training on new stainless steel pump range.
13 Wednesday	9.30 Frank Wright, Plantnorm. Follow up quote. 11.30 Jeff Bridges, I.C.D. Cold call - get general information on any future projects. 3.00. Paul Manning, Trapto Steel. Use our M40 in new plant in Aberdeen?
14 Thursday	9.30 ↓ Fisher and Welbeck. (See maintenance engineers before meeting if possible.) 10.00 Meeting: Sid Fisher, Ken Lockhart, Barry Lomax. <u>Get</u> order for complete Claycross project. THE BIG ONE !! GO GET IT BOY !!
15 Friday	Telephone calls : follow up all outstanding quotes.
16 Saturday 17 Sunday	Birmingham - Caroline + ? wedding Cancel golf with Martin.

The Findorp role-play

Aim: To practise the language of negotiation
Roles: John Morrison and Laurence Kale
Scene: A meeting to discuss the job at Gruber Industrial Pumps

Imagine John Morrison has not fallen ill. He has received the letter from Laurence Kale (page 47) and decides to try to negotiate better terms for himself. Decide what he wants: a better basic salary, higher commission, longer holidays, private medical insurance or less time away from home.

Decide how much Kale can afford to offer and what he thinks Morrison will accept. Add any details you think are realistic. Try to reach a compromise that suits you both.

The Findorp written assignment

Imagine that you have heard that C R Industries of Liverpool are setting up a large chemical plant in the north of England soon. Write a letter in answer to their telex (page 49) and enclose the literature they have requested. Unfortunately you are too busy to call personally with this literature immediately but make sure your letter interests them in your product and gets you a personal interview with the buyer soon.

Here are some phrases that you may find useful:

Please find enclosed . . .

I would like the opportunity to { visit . . . / quote for . . . / talk over . . . }

Let me draw your attention to . . .

You will find our { prices / terms } very competitive.

5

THE RECRUITMENT FILE

The situation

You are Joy Cooper, the personnel officer of a charity called 'House the Homeless'. House the Homeless works to improve the conditions of homeless people in Britain. The organisation also brings the results of its own research to the notice of the public and the government, to enlist support for its work.

Since 1973, House the Homeless has employed a small team of Liaison Officers to visit schools and colleges to explain the work and aims of the organisation. Recently one of the Schools Liaison Officers handed in his notice because he found that long hours of travelling between schools did not leave him enough time to be with his wife and child.

It is now your job to arrange interviews to select a replacement for this member of staff. On the following pages you will find the file on the problem. Look through it carefully and decide on *two* candidates to be invited for interview.

EMPLOYEE SPECIFICATION

Title of Post Schools Liaison Officer (South of England)

Qualities wanted	
1. Physical	Good health record. Smart appearance. If possible aged around 30.
2. Attainments	Education: University degree or secondary teacher training certificate or equivalent. Work experience: Evidence of success in secondary or tertiary level teaching or in P.R. department of private company or charity. If possible evidence of ability to organise own time. If possible evidence of some experience of officework.
3. Abilities	Good speaker. Car driver. If possible clean licence.
4. Disposition	Confidence. Friendly and persuasive personality. Interest in and awareness of the work of H the H and other organisations working for the homeless. If possible evidence of leadership e.g. at school or college or sports club. If possible evidence of commitment to aims of H the H and similar charities e.g. voluntary work experience.
5. Circumstances	Willingness to be away from home overnight from time to time and work irregular hours. Home in South or willing to move to area. Home telephone(if possible) If possible married, with stable family life.

JOB SPECIFICATION

Title of Post Schools Liaison Officer (South of England)

Department Education

Location

Based at headquarters Amersham, Bucks. Much travelling required to schools throughout the South.

Responsible to

Ms Norma Leighton,
Education Officer.

Purpose of Post

To improve the awareness and understanding of secondary school students and teachers of H the H's work. Where possible to encourage active participation in H the H's fund raising activities by putting schools in touch with local organisers.

Responsibilities

1. Send out literature to all secondary schools in the South of England.

2. Plan lecture tours of schools both for him/herself and other part-time staff in the area.

3. Follow up queries on the work of H the H by personal visits or letter.

4. Keep a detailed record of schools visited.

5. Encourage support for local H the H projects by putting interested schools in touch with local organisers.

6. Research ways of stimulating interest in the work of H the H in schools.

7. Keep up-to-date his/her knowledge of H the H projects and the law as it affects the homeless.

Contacts

The Schools Liaison Officer is a member of a team of 5 SLO's who cover all the secondary schools in Britain. Regular meetings are held between SLO's. Reports are written for the Education Officer and weekly meetings are arranged between the SLO and the Education Officer. SLO's are occasionally required to attend other meetings relevant to their work.

Conditions

H.Q. at Amersham keeps office hours. The SLO shares an office there and has secretarial back-up. Most of his/her work will be done to suit the school timetable. Some evening and weekend work will be necessary, for which the SLO arranges to take time off in lieu. Holidays should be taken during school holiday periods.

Payment

Annual salary of £7,000. Possibility of paying slightly more for excellent applicant. Car and petrol allowance. Pension scheme.

Promotion Prospects

Promotion within the education department is strictly limited but promotion into other departments within H the H is possible.

HOUSE THE HOMELESS

Frank Fidelity C.B.E. (Chairman)

Trustees:
Lord Dornmouth
Brian Newbury
Samuel Samuelson
Felicity Morgan-Union
Camilla Humberjack
Frederica Sayers
Caroline Moon
Mathew Filbers M.P.
Sir Stephen Storridge

Director General: Andrew Peacecorn M.A.

5 West Hill,
Amersham,
Buckinghamshire
AM5 CV3

Telephone: 02403 5978
Telex: 533599 HOMER G
Cables: HOMER AMERSHAM

Charity Trust No.: 237085

September

Dear

.... has said you have agreed to act as a referee in his/her application for the post of Schools Liaison Officer with House the Homeless. Details of the post are enclosed.

Please would you answer the following questions:

1. How long have you known the applicant?

2. In what capacity? If in a work capacity please note his/her main responsibilities and his/her health record.

3. Have you always found the applicant to be honest and reliable?

4. Do you think he/she would be suitable for the above post?

5. Please give your full name, telephone number and profession.

Yours truly

Ms J Cooper
Personnel Officer

Memorandum

To Joy Cooper

From Norma Leighton

Date 19th August

From the dates you offered me I would prefer the interviews for the selection of the South of England Schools Liaison Officer to be held on September 30th.

I agree to your suggested interview panel: myself, you, John Baines from our southern region local organisers' committee and Paul Williams from the "Schools in Action" group.

As far as "any other points" are concerned I think we should definitely be careful about choosing someone who looks good at the interview but who has not got the right family circumstances to cope with the unsocial hours. However, how one finds out about such things I just do not know!

* If you are interested in my applicati[on]
I would appreciate it if you could intervi[ew]
me between now and Sept. 30th. as on
that date I begin my annual 4 month
stay in Iran.

APPLICATION FORM

Name Barry Thompson **Age** 35

Address 'The Willows', Woodside Lane, Mickleborough, E. Sussex.
107 Lanrifi, Teheran 91 (after Sept 30th*)

Home telephone 0227-43957 **Work telephone** 0227-39641

Do you suffer from any recurring illness or disability? If so, give details.

No

Education and Professional Training:

Dates	Institutions attended	Qualifications obtained
1964	Camberwell Grammar School	'A' level: Maths, Physics, Chemistry
1967	Hull University	Degree in Chemical Engineering
1974	Calcott Engineering Co.	Sales training course

History of Employment:

Dates	Name and address of employer	Main responsibilities	Salary
1968-74	Kandan Chemicals, Liverpool.	Worked with team of engineers setting up chemical plants.	£3-4,500
1974	Joined Calcott Engineering, Liverpool as salesman visiting companies here and abroad.		£5-6,250
1979	Promoted to Sales Manager, Middle East, controlled and trained staff of 23 salesmen, based in Teheran.		£9,500 + generous benefits

Do you have a current driving licence? **Any endorsements?**

Give details of your spare-time activities, include details of any clubs you have belonged to, any positions of responsibility held, and any voluntary work undertaken since leaving school.

I am a committed Christian and most of my spare time is spent in church activities or with my family.

Why are you applying for this post?

In 1978 I became a committed Christian and, although in an excellent position with my present firm, I have been looking for a job where I can improve people's lives and not only buy more goods for myself and my family. This post is ideal.

Give the names, addresses and occupations of two people who have agreed to give you a reference for this application.

Rev. Peter Barkleton
The Vicarage
St John's Church
Upper Mickleborough
East Sussex

Dr. Francis Jones
Calcott Engineering
Calcott House
Charles Street, London WC1
(Manager of Overseas Operations)

Signature Barry Thompson **Date** Sept. 6th

23rd September 198-

Reference for Mr Barry Thompson

Mr Thompson had given Dr Francis Jones as one of his referees for the post of Schools Liaison Officer. Dr Jones was on holiday until today and telephoned through this reference to save time:

'I have known Mr Barry Thompson for two years. I am his immediate superior in my post as Manager of Overseas Operations for Calcott Engineering, where Mr Thompson works as Sales Manager (Middle East). In this post he has trained and supervised a force of 20-25 salesmen. He has been entirely satisfactory in this post and completely trustworthy. I think he could do the job you describe, although he is used to a great deal of responsibility and pressure. His own health record has been good but he has had to take time away from his work when his wife has been ill recently.'

Reverend Peter Barkleton,
The Vicarage,
St John's,
Upper Mickleborough,
East Sussex KF4 TH5

House the Homeless,

Dear Ms Cooper,

Mr Thompson has been a worshipper at my church for about eighteen months. He is a thoroughly honest and trustworthy man who has put in much work for St. John's over that time. I know he has found working abroad rather difficult because of his family and religious commitments and I would be very pleased if he took up employment nearer home. I am sure he would be a great asset to your charity, just as he has proved to be to the church.

Yours sincerely,

P. Barkleton

15th September

School porter said Mr. Shawcross was abroad and could not be contacted before September 29th

APPLICATION FORM

Name STEPHEN GARETH WILLIAMS **Age** 29

Address 22b KING ALFRED ROAD, BRIGHTON

Home telephone BRIGHTON 478621 **Work telephone** BRIGHTON 493166

Do you suffer from any recurring illness or disability? If so, give details.

NO

Education and Professional Training:

Dates	Institutions attended	Qualifications obtained
64-71	VARIOUS INTERNATIONAL SCHOOLS ABROAD	6 GCE O-LEVELS 2 A-LEVELS
71-72	SORBONNE (PARIS UNIVERSITY)	
72-75	ABERYSTWYTH UNIVERSITY, WALES	FRENCH DEGREE
75-76	BRADLEY AND HUSK, PUBLISHERS, LONDON	TRAINING COURSE IN PUBLISHING

History of Employment:

Dates	Name and address of employer	Main responsibilities	Salary
75-76	BRADLEY AND HUSK PUBLISHERS	— FOLLOWED TRAINING COURSE IN ALL ASPECTS OF PUBLISHING	£2,500
76-77	KETTLETON SCHOOL, CAMBRIDGE	— TAUGHT GIRLS 11-15 FRENCH	£2,500
77-78	MAIDLEY NEWSPAPER GROUP, LONDON	— SOLD ADVERTISING SPACE	£2,700
78-79	CRANBALLS BOYS SCHOOL	— TAUGHT PHYSICAL EDUCATION	£4,100
79-	BRIGHTON HOUSE THE HOMELESS	— HAVE BEEN RUNNING FUND-RAISING ACTIVITIES FOR H. THE H. IN THIS AREA	£5,000

Do you have a current driving licence? YES **Any endorsements?** 2

Give details of your spare-time activities, include details of any clubs you have belonged to, any positions of responsibility held, and any voluntary work undertaken since leaving school.

RUGBY, CRICKET, SAILING. AMATEUR DRAMATICS. HAVE BELONGED TO VARIOUS SPORTS CLUBS AND OCCASIONALLY HELD RESPONSIBLE POSITIONS IN THEM. RAN SCHOOL PLAY AT KETTLETON SCHOOL AND CRANBALLS BOYS SCHOOL.

Why are you applying for this post?

I LIKE WORKING FOR H. THE H. BUT I FEEL I COULD BE BETTER USED IN SCHOOLS TALKING ABOUT H. THE H.'S WORK. I GET ON VERY WELL WITH SCHOOLCHILDREN AND I AM SURE I COULD GET THEM ORGANISED TO SUPPORT OUR WORK.

Give the names, addresses and occupations of two people who have agreed to give you a reference for this application.

JEREMY MOOREHOUSE,
DEPUTY DIRECTOR,
HOUSE THE HOMELESS,
AMERSHAM

RODNEY SHAWCROSS,
CRANBALLS SCHOOL,
CRANBALLS,
SURREY (HEAD OF HOUSE, HEAD OF PHYSICAL ED.)

Signature S.G. Williams **Date** SEPTEMBER 7th.

HOUSE THE HOMELESS

Internal Report

Subject ..... CONFIDENTIAL report on Stephen G Williams .....

Written by ..... J Moorhouse .....

For the attention of ..... Joy Cooper .....

Date ..... Sept 9 ..... Department .....

Stephen G Williams has worked for House the Homeless since August last year. During that time he has had the position of local organiser for the Brighton and Hove area. He has worked hard and well, making many new contacts and developing several fund-raising projects. He seems honest and reliable and would probably do the job of Schools Liaison Officer very well indeed, as he has a persuasive, informal friendly manner and seems to get on well with everyone. However, my only reservation is that he has only been with us a year and is just beginning to really build up his area. I would like to see him stay in his present post for another couple of years and if he is successful, then perhaps we should offer him some promotion. But that decision is not in my hands and I would not like to stand in the way of this man's advancement.

APPLICATION FORM

Name Frank Morel **Age** 28

Address 23 Suffolk Drive, Beaconsfield, near Amersham, Bucks.

Home telephone (04946) 537 **Work telephone** —

Do you suffer from any recurring illness or disability? If so, give details.

I am registered as disabled. I can get about very well in my wheelchair and have a special disabled person's car.

Education and Professional Training:

Dates	Institutions attended	Qualifications obtained
64–71	Kilmarnock Grammer School	8 O-Level passes 3 A-Level passes
71–74	Edinburgh University	BSc Honours in Chemistry (II i)
74–75	Leicester University, Education School.	Certificate in Education

History of Employment:

Dates	Name and address of employer	Main responsibilities	Salary
75–NOW	Beaconsfield Middle School	Teacher of general science subjects. Head of department since 1978.	£7,000

Do you have a current driving licence? Yes **Any endorsements?** No

Give details of your spare-time activities, include details of any clubs you have belonged to, any positions of responsibility held, and any voluntary work undertaken since leaving school.

I run a club for disabled teenagers in this area. I also take them camping each summer for a couple of weeks. In my spare-time I write children's books based on scientific discoveries or play the baroque flute.

Why are you applying for this post?

I would like to put my understanding of young people, education and the disadvantaged together to find an interesting job outside the classroom.

Give the names, addresses and occupations of two people who have agreed to give you a reference for this application.

Mr. C. Grace,
The Headmaster
Beaconsfield Middle School,
Amersham Rd.,
Beaconsfield, Bucks.

Prof. G. MacDonald,
Chemistry Department,
Univ. of Edinburgh,
Edinburgh.
(Professor of Chemistry)

Signature Frank Morel **Date** 8th September

BEACONSFIELD MIDDLE SCHOOL

Amersham Road, Beaconsfield, Bucks KL8 4TF
Telephone Beaconsfield 7630

Headmaster: Charles Grace MA (Oxon)

House the Homeless
5 West Hill
Amersham

22nd September

Dear Miss Cooper

In answer to your request for a report on one of our teachers, Mr Frank Morel, I can say that Mr Morel joined my staff as a Scale 1 teacher. He became head of the Science department in 1978. He now has responsibility for five members of staff. I have no reservation in telling you that he is a fine teacher and has done a great deal for the department and, indeed, the school in general. He is hard-working, punctual, enthusiastic and, most of all, gets on excellently with both staff and pupils. He is extremely intelligent and a good organiser. I think he would make a very good Schools Liaison Officer, although I hesitate to say this as the school would notice his loss. As far as his health record is concerned, his disability has caused the school no inconvenience although he has to have termly medical check-ups for his spine. He has always managed to accommodate these absences within the timetable without detriment to his work.

Yours sincerely

Charles Grace

Charles Grace

22nd September 198-

<u>Reference for Mr Frank Morel</u>

As Professor MacDonald had not replied to our letter asking for a written reference for the above applicant we telephoned him at home and received this information:

Mr Morel studied under Prof. MacDonald between 1971 and 1974. He was a capable and extrovert student. He was injured in a road accident in his final year and lost the use of both legs. He took his final examinations in hospital and did well to get a second class degree. He continued to be very outgoing and good-humoured although he had to give up his captaincy of the university rugby team. Professor MacDonald felt he would do the job of Schools Liaison Officer very well if he could overcome the obvious mobility problems. He added that he felt sure the applicant was honest and reliable.

X-On leave, would be available end of the month at 58 Canal St., Manchester 9.

APPLICATION FORM

Name Samantha Rees-Jones **Age** 31

Address 6, Palmero Mansions, Palmero Road
Highgate, London N6

Home telephone 01-242 9697 **Work telephone** 01-483 4751

Do you suffer from any recurring illness or disability? If so, give details.

No

Education and Professional Training:

Dates	Institutions attended	Qualifications obtained
60-68	Chelmsford College	4 'A' levels 10 'O' levels
68-71	Bristol University	Degree: BA Hons (1st class) German and Drama

History of Employment:

Dates	Name and address of employer	Main responsibilities	Salary
71-74	Volunteers Overseas	Teaching classes of village children all primary subjects	Subsistence Allowance
(74-79	Married, 2 children, lived in Thailand with diplomat husband - divorced)		
79-now	Help the Old	Part-time general office work helping to organise fund-raising campaigns for this national charity	approx. £4 per hr.

Do you have a current driving licence? Yes **Any endorsements?** No

Give details of your spare-time activities, include details of any clubs you have belonged to, any positions of responsibility held, and any voluntary work undertaken since leaving school. For voluntary work see above 71-74. I also did some voluntary visiting in Thai hospitals. My only position of responsibility was to be head-girl in 1973-4 at school. My hobbies are opera, theatre, amateur dramatics, playing the viola, cooking.

Why are you applying for this post?

Since my divorce I am anxious to start a career which will totally involve me and where my teaching and voluntary work experience will be useful. I feel House the Homeless is a very worthwhile charity that I would like to support actively.

Give the names, addresses and occupations of two people who have agreed to give you a reference for this application.

X Mr Colin Dee
Educational Representative
N. African Section
Volunteers Overseas
PO Box 42 London W1

Mrs Sandra Menzies
Education Officer
Help the Old
Falmouth House
Falmouth Square,
London W1.

Signature S. Rees-Jones

Date 7th Sept.

21st September 198-

Reference for Ms Samantha Rees-Jones

Mrs Sandra Menzies, Education Officer for Help the Old, telephoned through this report as she was in hospital:

'I have known Mrs Rees-Jones for twelve months. She works as a part-time helper in the offices of Help the Old where she does general office tasks and some administrative work connected with fund-raising campaigns. Her health record has been fine as far as I am aware. I believe she would be a splendid Schools Liaison Officer, in fact, I told her to apply for this post. She wants a full-time job and is too bright and enthusiastic to stay in an office all her life. She is a delightful girl, a beautiful speaker and has a winning personality.'

APPLICATION FORM

Name Jeffrey Marshall **Age** 30

Address 21, Wilford Avenue, Manchester 16.

Home telephone 061-574-3295 **Work telephone** —

Do you suffer from any recurring illness or disability? If so, give details.

No

Education and Professional Training:

Dates **Institutions attended** **Qualifications obtained**

After leaving South Manchester Grammar School with 2 A-Levels I trained as a teacher of the blind and worked at the Cheshire Memorial Home for the Blind until last year.

History of Employment:

Dates **Name and address of employer** **Main responsibilities** **Salary**

My salary as a teacher of the blind was £5,120. Last year the Home closed and I was made redundant. I have retrained on a government grant since then, as a woodwork and metalwork teacher. I have a job doing this in Manchester from September 25th, if I want it. In fact I would prefer to leave teaching as the prospects look very poor at present.

Do you have a current driving licence? Yes **Any endorsements?** No

Give details of your spare-time activities, include details of any clubs you have belonged to, any positions of responsibility held, and any voluntary work undertaken since leaving school.

I was captain of the fencing club at school. At College I ran the students' newspaper. At the Home for the Blind I organised a lot of social evening and weekend activities on a voluntary basis. My main hobby is listening to jazz.

Why are you applying for this post?

See above. I have a lot of experience with young people. I am willing to move, with my wife and child, to Amersham.

Give the names, addresses and occupations of two people who have agreed to give you a reference for this application.

Mark Crawley,
c/o Manchester College of Education
Wythenshawe,
Manchester.
(Tutor on my retraining course)

Sir Gerald Smiley,
The Deanery,
Poldark Garden Lane,
Wilmslow, Cheshire,
(ex-head of Cheshire Home for Blind)

Signature Jeff Marshall

Date 7th September

The Deanery,
Poldark Garden Lane,
Wilmslow,
Cheshire.

14th September

Ms. J. Cooper
Personnel Officer,
House the Homeless,
5 West Hill,
Amersham,
Buckinghamshire.

Dear Ms. Cooper,

I have no hesitation in recommending Mr. Jeffrey Marshall for the post you wrote to me about. He was a first-rate teacher when the Cheshire Memorial Home for the Blind was open and I was very sorry to see him made redundant. He joined my staff in 1971 and was a most reliable man. He joined in a lot of outside school activities with the pupils and worked extremely hard.

Yours sincerely,

G. Smiley

Gerald Smiley

23rd September 198-

Reference for Mr Jeffrey Marshall

As Mark Crawley had not replied to our letter asking for a written reference he was telephoned. The following notes were taken:

Mr Crawley has known the candidate for a year. The candidate was a student of his on a retraining scheme at Manchester College of Education. The course finished in June this year. He could not comment on his health record, his honesty or his reliability. He did not wish to say whether he felt the candidate suitable for the post as he thought it was the candidate's duty to take up a teaching post he had been retained for at government expense.

APPLICATION FORM

Name Sally Miller **Age** 26

Address 52 Chapel Hill Drive, Finchley, London

Home telephone 01-431-0020 **Work telephone** —

Do you suffer from any recurring illness or disability? If so, give details.

No

Education and Professional Training:

Dates	Institutions attended	Qualifications obtained
1972-1975	London School of Economics (University of London)	Degree (2nd. Class) in Sociology.

History of Employment:

Dates	Name and address of employer	Main responsibilities	Salary
1975	Worked for British Metallics as a public relations officer. This involved me in helping to make films about the work of the company and then taking these films round to schools explaining the company's policies. When British Metallics was taken over by English Steelworks I was promoted to education officer, preparing work-packs on the industry.		£2,500 - £6,500

Do you have a current driving licence? No **Any endorsements?** —

Give details of your spare-time activities, include details of any clubs you have belonged to, any positions of responsibility held, and any voluntary work undertaken since leaving school.

I play badminton and enjoy sailing at the weekends. The only voluntary work I can claim to have done is organize a seaside trip for spastics last summer through the company's social club.

Why are you applying for this post? I love the work in the education/P.R. Department of English Steelworks except that I am getting bored with talking about steel-making! I would really love to join a worthwhile charity such as House the Homeless and I think I could do the job very well.

Give the names, addresses and occupations of two people who have agreed to give you a reference for this application.

Mr. S. Pembroke
Head of Public Relations
English Steelworks
E.S. House, London WC1

Dr. K. Falls,
(Tutor in Sociology)
L.S.E.
Aldwych London WC2

Signature Sally Miller **Date** 8th Sept.

ENGLISH STEELWORKS

P.O. Box 4,
E.S. House,
London WC1R 4FP

Telephone: 01-522 4646/7
Telex: 464646 Engst E
Cables: Engst London

Your ref:

Our ref:
SP/JL/13

Ms J Cooper
Personnel Officer
House the Homeless
5, West Hill
Amersham
Bucks

13.9.8-

<u>Confidential Reference on Ms Sally Miller</u>

Dear Ms Cooper

Here are the answers to the questions put in your letter of the 11th September:

1. I have known Ms Miller since 1977.

2. I am her immediate superior in the Public Relations/Education Department of English Steelworks. Ms Miller's main responsibilities include researching then writing workpacks for secondary schools to illustrate the work of English Steelworks, its effect on the community and its policies for the future. These workpacks comprise boardgames, group discussion and problem-solving exercises and visual aids for the teacher's use in the science laboratory. In addition Ms Miller occasionally visits schools and speaks to science and economics teachers to get their reactions to the materials she produces. On three occasions recently Ms Miller gave short lectures on the steel-making industry at careers conventions for sixth-form leavers.

   Ms Miller has had 4 days of absence since joining this department.

3. Ms Miller is perfectly honest and reliable to my knowledge.

4. Yes, with some training of course.

I should add on behalf of my department that we would be very sorry to lose Ms Miller.

Yours sincerely

S. Pembroke

Stephen Pembroke
Head of Public Relations, English Steelworks

57 Bishops Hill,
Islington,
London, N7.
15th September

Ms. J. Cooper,
Personnel Officer,
H the H,
5 West Hill,
Amersham.

Dear Ms Cooper,

Ms. Sally Miller was a bright and ambitious student when she studied under me at the London School of Economics and Political Science from '72-5. I am sure she will do very well in any career she chooses. The post with you sounds just right.

Yours truly,

Kenneth Falls

GENERAL

A UNIVERSITY OF
OGY

FFICER

e-mentioned position in the

ified in the fields of building
e extensive experience in all
t of plans through to completion
rative and staff supervisory
a.

ll buildings matters including
ultants, administrative control,
n of works and settlement. He
nce Engineer on maintenance

lued at over K20M. and it is
t a moderate pace for some

er benefits include a gratuity of
riation fares, leave fares, for the
ths of service, settling-in and out
, education fares and assistance
ry continuation and medical

riculum vitae together with the
should be received by the
y of Technology, P.O. Box 793,

HOUSE THE HOMELESS
wish to appoint
SCHOOLS LIAISON OFFICER

We are looking for an excellent communicator who wants to help fight the problem of homelessness in Britain. He or she must be able to organize his or her own timetable, travel extensively in the South of England, create interest in the aims of House the Homeless in secondary schools by visits and lectures, and liaise with the other Schools Liaison Officers and the Education Department to draw up educational policies. We can offer:

- a worthwhile career
- a salary of £7,000 p.a.
- a car and petrol allowance
- 6 weeks holiday a year

If you are between 25 and 40 and think you have the experience to take on this challenging post, write for details and application form to: Ms J. Cooper, Personnel Dept., House the Homeless, 5 West Hill, Amersham, Bucks.

THE PAPUA N

Applications are invit

Applicants should be
and/or civil engineerin
aspects of building wor
of a project togeth

The appointee will be
preparation of briefs, e
and site supervision th
will work in association

Current buildings and ser
anticipated that develop

Initial contract period
24% taxed at 2%, appoi
staff member and fami
allowances, six weeks p
towards school fees, f

Detailed applications (tw
names and addresses
Registrar, Papua New

Applicants resident in th

Sunday Times Aug. 30th
Guardian Sept. 2nd.
Times Educational Supplement Sept. 3rd.

The recruitment role-play

Aim: To practise asking detailed questions and answering them convincingly
Roles: Joy Cooper, Norma Leighton, John Baines, Paul Williams and the two short-listed candidates
Scene: Interviews for the post of Schools Liaison Officer

The panel are ready to interview the two short-listed candidates. Each member of the panel should check the applications of the candidates and prepare searching questions about points they are unsure of. Meanwhile the two candidates should prepare questions about the job so that they can be sure it is what they want. The candidates should be as convincing as they can if they want the job. Make up any other details which are necessary in the interview. The panel may want a short meeting before the interviews, but the candidates should not talk to each other. After the interviews the panel should decide who will be offered the job.

The recruitment written assignment

Write a brief letter to the unsuccessful applicants for the post. A general letter will be sent to them all.

Here are some phrases you may find useful:

I regret to inform you that . . .
Thank you for your interest in . . .
After careful consideration (of) . . .